Tul

100 Years of
Weather
Twentieth Century in Pictures

100 Years of
Weather
Twentieth Century in Pictures

AMMONITE
PRESS

PRESS
ASSOCIATION
Images

First Published 2009 by
Ammonite Press
an imprint of AE Publications Ltd,
166 High Street, Lewes, East Sussex BN7 1XU

Text copyright Ammonite Press
Images copyright Press Association Images
Copyright in the work Ammonite Press

ISBN 978-1-906672-24-9

British Cataloguing in Publication Data. A catalogue
record of this book is available from the British Library.

Editor: Andy Stansfield
Series editor: Paul Richardson
Picture research: Press Association Images
Design: Gravemaker + Scott

Colour reproduction by GMC Reprographics
Printed and bound by Kyodo Nation Printing, Thailand

Page 2: This search party
was sent out into the Surrey
countryside to locate a
charabanc that had been
reported as missing between
Godstone and Redhill. It
was discovered completely
submerged beneath drifting
snow.
30th December, 1927

Page 5: A day at the
seaside, Sussex style,
complete with canvas
changing huts on the shingle
beach at the resort of Hove.
1st August, 1910

Page 6: Motorists are
warned – perhaps
unnecessarily – that the
River Trent has overflowed,
flooding the highway and
neighbouring fields at
Twyford, Derbyshire.
23rd January, 1959

Introduction

The weather is a topic that opens more conversations in Britain than any other. For an island people in the direct path of a wide variety of weather systems crossing the Atlantic, this fact is not surprising: the country's weather can change from hour to hour and in places it is said that all four seasons can be experienced in a single day.

Much of the historic information regarding weather is anecdotal and derived from literature, which means that it is necessarily subjective and cannot be relied upon for absolute accuracy. But scientific meteorological recording goes back further than many realise – rainfall in Britain has been recorded on a daily basis since 1766 and provides the longest continuous set of weather data in the world. Many recording stations have now been established across the land, and out at sea, to provide meteorologists with the comprehensive data needed to aid forecasting.

But inevitably forecasters can get it wrong, sometimes with terrible consequences. The catastrophic flooding of eastern regions in 1953, causing many lives to be lost, wasn't anticipated by meteorologists who failed to understand the picture that was unfolding. On another infamous occasion, the 15th of October 1987, the evening forecast light-heartedly dismissed rumours of hurricane force winds: just hours later trees were uprooted, buildings destroyed and chaos gripped southern England in a night of unparalleled devastation.

Although situated in temperate latitudes Britain's weather can be extreme, as some of the images in this book illustrate. Fluctuations in temperature range from a high of 38.5 degrees down to minus 27.2 degrees. The highest wind speed recorded is 142mph, while the sunniest place on record is Eastbourne with 383.9 hours of sunshine in a single month during July 1911. But the most frequent subject of conversation is probably rain, and the most rainfall experienced in a 24-hour period was a fraction short of 11 inches in 1955: what is most surprising is that it occurred in Dorset in July.

Fortunately the story of events such as these in the islands' towns, countryside and extensive coastline has been diligently recorded over the years, allowing us to see this history for ourselves. These pictures also tell us a great deal about the communities in which we live and work and in the pages of this book, through photographs selected from the vast archives of The Press Association, can be found a rare insight into the special relationship that the British enjoy with their weather.

Bathed in sunshine, the
colourful spectacle of the
annual Henley Regatta
unfolds before throngs of
spectators.
6th July, 1907

Early June weather is warm enough to draw people to the beach at Yarmouth, but sea temperatures are still chilly enough to deter most from bathing.
1st June, 1908

USA's Ralph Rose in action in the rain, on the way to winning his second successive Olympic Gold in the Shot Put at the 1908 London Olympics.
16th July, 1908

Great Britain's Charles
Bartlett comes home first to
win Gold in the 100km track
event at White City in the
1908 London Olympics.
18th July, 1908

During the 1908 London Olympics, rowing events were held
at Henley-on-Thames. Great Britain, represented by the
Leander Club, beat Belgium to win Gold in the final of the
Coxed Eights.
31st July, 1908

People enjoying the sun on
the cliffs close to the seaside
town of Folkestone in Kent.
1st July, 1909

Mrs Ashton Harrison at Ascot races. Racing at the Berkshire venue was first envisioned by Queen Anne in 1711 while out riding from Windsor Castle.
1910

The Duke and Duchess of Beaufort at Richmond Horse Show, which came into being as the result of a chance encounter at a cricket match and flourished for 75 years.
1910

Margate began to develop as a resort in the second half
of the 18th century. The sea-bathing machine – a wheeled
contraption that could be moved to the shoreline to allow
bathing privacy – was invented by a Margate man, Benjamin
Beale. Perhaps the most noticeable thing about this image is
that everyone is fully dressed.
1st August, 1910

Facing page: Throngs
of race-goers attend
the Epsom Derby,
the boater undoubtedly
being the gentlemen's
headgear of choice.
June, 1911

A variety of elegant high-society guests, including the actress Gertie Miller, attend a garden party for actors and actresses.
1st August, 1911

Margaret and David Lloyd
George camping at the
base of the 2570ft (783m)
mountain Moel Hebog, which
broods over the small North
Wales town of Beddgelert.
1913

A bathing scene at Margate
– with bathing caps being
the order of the day.
1st May, 1914

Facing page: Tea-time
scene at Ranelagh Gardens,
purchased by a syndicate
in 1741 to provide attractive
public gardens for Chelsea.
The venue now forms part
of the grounds of Chelsea
Hospital and is the site of the
annual Chelsea Flower Show.
1913

Crowds enjoy the late May sunshine at the Epsom Derby, won by *Durbar II* ridden by Matt MacGee, unaware of the conflict which was to follow the assassination of the heir to the Austro-Hungarian throne just one month later.

31st May, 1914

The very latest in bathing caps, costumes and wraps, as designed for Harrods, are seen in this Margate snapshot captured for Pathe Frere's weekly film review for women.
20th May, 1921

The Honourable Timothy
Bowes-Lyon and the
Honourable Nancy Moira
Bowes-Lyon, twin children
of Lord and Lady Glamis,
picking flowers in the
spring at Yew Tree House,
Westfield, Sussex.
20th April, 1923

The Duke and Duchess of York, later to become Queen
Elizabeth and King George VI, at a Fresh Air Fund For
Children event in Epping Forest. The Duchess (née Lady
Elizabeth Bowes-Lyon) tries her luck at the coconut shy.
19th July, 1923

On a pleasant autumn day Lord Fitzwarine Chichester (C) relaxes on a park bench with 'Buns' (L), the legendary cricketer Charles Inglis Thornton who played in over 200 first class matches for no fewer than 22 different teams.

29th September, 1923

Two bathers enjoy the
summer sunshine in what
appears a rather precarious
situation while on holiday at
Cowes on the Isle of Wight.
25th July, 1925

The Minister of Health,
the Honourable Neville
Chamberlain, enjoys a walk
in Hyde Park with his wife
Anne on a glorious day in
early spring.
8th March, 1926

Crowds flock to the Sussex
seaside resort of Eastbourne
to enjoy the Easter sunshine.
3rd April, 1926

Normal deliveries of food and other supplies to the isolated
inhabitants of St. Kilda, the tiny and most westerly island
of the Outer Hebrides, are interrupted by storms, so
the residents have to rely on a catch of fulmars to keep
themselves going. Today the fulmar is a protected species
and individual birds may live for 80 years.
3rd September, 1926

A trip to the shops presents
all the challenges of a
polar expedition for these
residents of Keston in Kent.
29th December, 1927

On a crisp winter morning in the capital, Londoners are out in force for fresh air and exercise in Hyde Park.
5th January, 1928

Facing page: Paving blocks in Grosvenor Road, London, scattered by the force of floodwaters.
7th January, 1928

On the night of 6th January the flood tide was six feet higher than predicted in central London. Fourteen people drowned in basement flats while 4,000 were made homeless. This boat was washed up onto Page Street in Westminster.

7th January, 1928

The summer of 1928 saw a shortage of fresh water,
a situation exploited by this entrepreneur who is selling
drinking water at a halfpenny per pail at Docking in Norfolk.
30th August, 1928

A small boy wrapped up
warmly in hat and scarf in
The Rows, Great Yarmouth.
1st October, 1928

Kingsway, London, and the
old *Stoll Picture Theatre*,
opened in 1911 as the
London Opera House
then renamed after being
purchased by Oswald Stoll
in 1916.
6th January, 1929

This airborne girl sledges wildly
down a slope on Hampstead
Heath, the most popular and
accessible location in London
for winter sports.
31st January, 1929

A heavy snowfall on
Hampstead Heath brings out
Londoners and their sledges
in the winter sunshine.
31st January, 1929

Arctic scenes along the
River Trent as blocks
of broken ice litter the
landscape.
31st January, 1929

Facing page: Fun in the sun
by the river at Walton-on-
Thames.
25th May, 1929

Facing page: Seventeen years before the bikini was launched onto the fashion scene, these girls in their one-piece bathing costumes enjoy the atmosphere at the Dobb Weir Carnival in Hertfordshire.
6th August, 1929

Thick fogs known as *pea-soupers* were commonplace in London due to industrial air pollution and the use of coal fires for domestic heating. The young, elderly and infirm suffered respiratory ailments when conditions were at their worst.
1st March, 1932

Facing page: Floods in Surrey force this resident and her canaries to make for higher ground in Halliford.
4th May, 1932

Royal Ascot, held every summer in Berkshire, is renowned for ladies' fashions in general and hats in particular.
17th June, 1932

The scene at open air baths
at Kennington Park, where
south London residents seek
relief from a heat wave.
10th August, 1932

Sunbathing in the grounds
of a London day nursery.
Heliotherapy – sunbathing
for health – enjoyed
considerable popularity in
the 1930s and was regarded
as a public health measure.
12th September, 1932

London children at the
Dockland Settlement Day
Nursery in Canning Town
enjoy the luxury of taking
their lessons outside in
the sunshine.
12th September, 1932

Neville Chamberlain, Chancellor of the Exchequer, on the way to present his second budget to the House of Commons, with his own umbrella tightly furled as he is protected from the elements.

1st April, 1933

Some landscape features, such as the village pond, are considered quintessentially English and evoke visions of idyllic summer days. This example is at Potten End in Hertfordshire.
24th June, 1933

Spring flower shows, hotbeds of competition, are important fixtures on the calendar in rural areas. This grower carefully tends her exhibit at a horticultural show in Hertfordshire.
17th March, 1934

At this farm in Spalding,
Lincolnshire, daffodils
are picked for shipping to
markets and florists all over
the country.
13th April, 1934

Kaye Earnest Donsky, better known as Kaye Don, powers through Brooklands' puddles. A month later his accompanying mechanic, Francis Taylor, was killed during practice on the Isle of Man. Because the practice session had officially ended, Don was found guilty of manslaughter and served four months' imprisonment, effectively ending his career.

28th April, 1934

Lythe, near Whitby in Yorkshire, during heavy snowfall. It had been suggested that National Parks should be established for King George V's Silver Jubilee in this year, but instead more playing fields were built and it wasn't until 1952 that Lythe found itself part of the North Yorkshire Moors National Park.

17th May, 1935

Ice-cream bicycles were operated in London by Walls from the early 1920s, when Cecil Rodd coined the famous slogan: 'Stop Me and Buy One'. By the late 1950s most had disappeared as Walls invested instead in freezers for their stockists' shops.

26th August, 1935

Crowds throng the London
streets in damp and foggy
weather, Blackfriars being
packed with umbrellas.
29th January, 1936

Scenes such as this, during the Second Test between England and Australia, make one wonder if practically everybody read a daily newspaper at that time – or whether they were purchased specifically in case of rain.
27th June, 1938

Facing page: Children enjoy a snowball fight in a Trafalgar Square devoid of both adults and pigeons.
7th November, 1938

Bob Ansell ploughs through standing water at Brooklands during what proved to be the last race meeting held at the historic circuit. The race was won by Prince Birabongse Bhanutej Bhanubandh, known affectionately as B Bira, a member of the Thai Royal family.
6th May, 1939.

The Duke of Gloucester chats with one of the farm workers while helping with the wartime harvest at his farm, Barnwell Manor near Oundle, Northamptonshire.
29th August, 1944

The war in Europe is over and some sense of normality is beginning to return. Servicemen and women are eager to taste life's pleasures, such as enjoying a beer while watching the first day's play in the Third Victory Test against the Australian Services XI at Lord's.

14th July, 1945

ATS girls as they leave their
headquarters in Hastings,
Sussex, after a substantial
fall of snow has dressed the
trees in white.
27th February, 1946

A motorist is given a
helping hand as he runs
into difficulties with a slight
gradient on the Warlington
to Westerham Hill road in
Surrey.
3rd March, 1946

A line-up of lovely ladies soak up the sun at Butlins Holiday Camp in Skegness, as the site returns to peacetime duties after spending the war as HMS Royal Arthur – which the German navy twice claimed to have sunk!

21st June, 1946

A couple relax on Bournemouth's sun-soaked beach wearing traditional British headgear for protection against the elements: a newspaper and a knotted handkerchief.
12th July, 1946

Torrential rain proved too
much for drains to cope
with, forcing water up
through road surfaces
in this Hampstead street.
26th July, 1946

Torquay's wet and windy promenade is strewn with the wreckage of hundreds of deckchairs after autumn storms swept the south coast.

20th September, 1946

Facing page; As part of the post-war regeneration of manufacturing industry, the Victoria and Albert Museum in London holds the *Britain Can Make It* exhibition to promote excellence in British product design, including this display of umbrellas.
23rd September, 1946

The first day of a scheduled tour match between Australia and Marylebone Cricket Club brings a familiar problem: rain. Major Howard, the MCC's team manager (far L) along with Yardley, Hammond and Edrich, look hopefully skyward to judge whether conditions are likely to improve.
8th November, 1946

On a foggy night along the Great West Road an Automobile Association patrolman directs traffic near Cranford, Middlesex, with the help of the Fog Flare Service.
12th December, 1946

Facing page: One of the worst winters on record: streets are covered in snow in December but far worse weather is to come in the following two months.
19th December, 1946

The Mall: A solitary figure walking along the snow-bound avenue keeps her umbrella up to protect against thawing snow dripping from the trees.
19th December, 1946

A wintry scene in Trafalgar Square, London, when heavy snow fell on the capital. The severe weather caused real hardship, compounded by post-war shortages of food and fuel.
6th January, 1947

100 Years of Weather • Twentieth Century in Pictures

Facing page: A policeman maintains a lonely vigil in a deserted Trafalgar Square with the lions of Nelson's Column.
9th February, 1947

During one of the coldest months on record, overnight temperatures at Kew Botanic Gardens climbed above freezing just twice in four weeks, and minus 20 degrees was recorded as far south as Essex. This was one of only around 25 occasions in history when the Thames froze over.
27th February, 1947

Traffic chaos in Oxford Street, one of London's most famous
shopping thoroughfares, during the rush hour when only
one side of the road could be used by traffic owing to the
treacherous snow and ice.
6th March, 1947

Seventy-mile-per-hour winds
changed the landscape of
London, bringing down trees
across the capital. This
particular example is in Acacia
Road, St John's Wood.
17th March, 1947

Heroic efforts are made, in extremely dangerous conditions, to fill a breach in the north bank of the Little Ouse near Hockwold in Norfolk. Rapidly thawing snow combined with heavy rain brought extensive flooding to East Anglia: mobile canteens ferried up to 1,000 meals a day to those attempting to bolster weakened flood defences.
20th March, 1947

Facing page: Gales leave havoc in their wake across southern England, such as the wreckage of what had been the home of the Gerrard family in Fentiman Road, south west London. Fortunately the occupants were enjoying a drink in a local pub when the house was destroyed.
17th March, 1947

A motorcyclist leaves
a wake on Birdcage Walk:
London experienced
widespread flooding
following thunderstorms.
27th June, 1947

Four corvettes are designated to maintain positions in the Atlantic, on weather observation duties. The first of these, *HMS Marguerite*, is re-christened as Ocean Weather Ship *Weather Observer*. Able Seaman Potter is seen here as the ship prepares for a seven day journey to 53°50'N 18°40'W and its first 28-day stint.

31st July, 1947

Adults and children on their way to the Kent hop fields in
the summer sunshine. The hop-picking season was both
a source of extra income and a welcome break for those
struggling to make ends meet in the lean post-war years.
15th August, 1947

RAF meteorologists at Uxbridge Weather Station prepare to release a weather balloon that will record changes in the atmosphere while its course is plotted by a theodolite operator (L).
25th August, 1947

Facing page: An AA motorcycle patrolman renders assistance as a bus and several cars struggle through a snowstorm between London and Maidstone.
21st February, 1948

An aerial view of the Welsh Bridge area of Shrewsbury after serious flooding of the Severn and Wye rivers. Streets to the left of the bridge are completely flooded and impassable.
16th January, 1948

A group of dancing girls from the Windmill Theatre improve their 'can-can' technique on a London rooftop, while their colleagues make the most of the opportunity to improve their tans.
15th May, 1948

Facing page: Holidaymakers sunbathe at Butlins Holiday Camp at Skegness. For most, this will be their first proper holiday since before the war.
6th June, 1948

100 Years of Weather • Twentieth Century in Pictures

Facing page: A lone optimist at Wimbledon remains in his seat for the Men's Singles, umbrella raised but ready should play resume when the rain finally stops.
12th June, 1948

London's post-war Olympic Games, the first summer Olympics for 12 years, was a wet affair. As the Decathlon's 1500 metre race unfolds, Argentina's Enrique Kistenmacher (432) leads the way through the puddles.
6th August, 1948

As wind and rain strip the autumn colour from the trees in
St James' Park in London, there is always someone on hand
to sweep up the leaves.
19th October, 1948

A double-decker bus, travelling from Worthing to Brighton, crashed through a bridge into the Adur river, trapping 25 people inside. The fact that it was low tide probably saved the passengers from drowning.
2nd January, 1949

Winter sports on a frozen Wimbledon Common Pond. Even though three people fell through the ice, skaters were not deterred.
29th January, 1950

Facing page: A London policeman controls the flow of traffic during a New Year's Day snowstorm while others stay at home in the warm, nursing hangovers and listening to the Ink Spots. They would finish the week at Number 1 with *You're Breaking My Heart* at a time when the chart was based on sales of sheet-music, not records.
1st January, 1950

Officials of the Royal Meteorological Society attach a
radio transmitter to a weather balloon to test atmospheric
conditions at 30,000 feet above the Earth, as part of the
Society's 100th anniversary. Three years earlier and
5,000 miles to the west, a similar balloon was the official
explanation of the most famous UFO incident in history, near
the town of Roswell, New Mexico.
27th March, 1950

A small girl peers intently
into one of the many tulips
providing spring colour
in Hyde Park.
21st April, 1950

An almost mythical, English spring scene as people watch a cricket match on the village green of Frenchay.
26th April, 1950

Bowed under the weight of its 'blossom' of snow is this cherry tree at West Wickham, Kent, after the previous night's heavy snowfall.
26th April, 1950

A number of tornadoes occur every year in Britain, most being limited in size and short-lived. They usually occur in conjunction with violent thunderstorms, caused by powerful swirling air currents within the cloud mass which form a funnel like that seen here near Linslade.

21st May, 1950

Tornado damage in the village of Linslade near Leighton Buzzard, with village baker Mr Tysom clearing debris from his wrecked bakery. Hundreds of houses were damaged across Buckinghamshire and Bedfordshire as the late afternoon phenomenon wreaked havoc along a 66 mile path for over two hours, making it the longest lasting tornado in Europe.

22nd May, 1950

Young women bathe at Endell Street Open Air Pool, during hot weather. By this time the bikini, daringly introduced in July 1946 by French fashion designers and named after Bikini Atoll, where nuclear tests had been conducted, was well on the way to becoming commonplace.

26th May, 1950

Margaret Hardy plotting observations on a weather chart as they are received in the Central Forecasting Office of the British Meteorological Service at Dunstable.
12th July, 1950

Aubrey Taylor of Durley Hill Farm, near Keynsham in Gloucestershire, uses a horse and trap to venture out into the flooded fields to rescue his sheep in the worst floods the West Country had known for years.
21st November, 1950

An Automobile Association
motorcycle patrolman digs
a car out of a ditch after it
skidded on the ice-bound,
snow-covered Hog's Back
Road near Puttenham
crossroads, Guildford.
15th December, 1950

The New Year is heralded
by grim scenes such as this,
with dark skies, wind and
slush as a tram makes its
way along the Embankment
during a snowstorm.
January, 1951

Wind drives snow almost
horizontally to fall on
traffic in Farringdon Street,
London.
January, 1951

Men and women alike queue for fur coats in the New Year
sale at Swears and Wells in the West End of London, a sign,
perhaps, that the post-war economy is beginning to recover.
January, 1951

Overturned railway wagons
in a siding at Dover harbour,
blown over by violent gales
which swept Britain's south
coast.
14th March, 1951

Molly Beavan of Bristol bottle-feeding young lambs in the pastoral setting of a blossom-filled orchard in Sandford, Somerset.
19th May, 1951

The Oxford University crew
row out into a blizzard,
at the 98th annual Boat
Race against Cambridge
University.
29th March, 1952

The Lynmouth disaster. Two weeks of heavy rain had left
Exmoor saturated when a 21 hour downpour – 11 inches
of rain of which half fell in just five hours – swelled the East
Lyn and West Lyn rivers. Draining through Lynmouth to the
sea, their combined torrents became a wall of water which
demolished homes, resulting in 34 deaths. Supposed links
with cloud-seeding trials were subsequently disproved.
17th August, 1952

This date saw Britain's worst natural disaster in living memory as freak weather conditions funnelled a massive storm surge southwards towards the English Channel, affecting East Anglia down to the Thames estuary. Here a woman is carried along flooded streets in the Wisbech Road area of King's Lynn.

1st February, 1953

A lone rescue worker sculls a boat through a flooded street in Clay in North Norfolk. The village suffered with other parts of Norfolk and the east coast in widespread flooding. Lincolnshire suffered the first fatalities on land when over 40 people drowned as 20ft waves crashed through flood defences.

1st February, 1953

Facing page: Members of the public are helped by firemen pulling a small boat in flood-stricken Canvey Island, Essex. Canvey's floods occurred overnight, greatly increasing the loss of life. Although it is the east coast floods which are generally remembered, the storm started off the Irish coast causing the loss of 130 lives in the sinking of the ferry *Princess Victoria*.

2nd February, 1953

An aerial view showing servicemen mending a breach in the sea wall at Canvey Island, the Thames estuary holiday resort most overwhelmed in the flood disaster. The Netherlands' dykes were also severely breached, causing over 1,800 deaths.
2nd February, 1953

Cattle cling perilously to a tiny scrap of dry land amid an ocean of destruction as flood waters from the Thames estuary continue to rise. The floods were responsible for the deaths of an estimated 50,000 animals.
2nd February, 1953

The Beach Hotel at Sutton-on-Sea on the Lincolnshire coast, some two miles south of the popular resort of Mablethorpe, provides a graphic illustration of how severe the floods were, even in the north of the affected area.

2nd February, 1953

The last inhabitants being compulsorily evacuated by police, troops and emergency services from Canvey Island where more than a hundred people are known to have died. The total death toll in Britain was 307.

2nd February, 1953

Meteorologist George
Cowling is chosen by
the BBC to liven up their
television presentation of the
weather report and forecast.
Here he studies a chart at
the Meteorological Office in
Victory House, Kingsway,
London.
5th January, 1954

George Cowling, in one of his first appearances as the presenter of *Weather Chart* for the BBC from Lime Grove Studios, London. When Cowling once mentioned in a forecast that the following day would be good for drying the washing, he was reprimanded for frivolity.
11th January, 1954

Admiral Nelson's flagship,
HMS Victory, covered in
snow at its dry berth in
Portsmouth Dockyard.
26th January, 1954

A spectacular curtain of icicles was witnessed at Harwood, near Bolton, as a big freeze continued due to an anticyclone over Scandinavia, bringing biting easterly winds to parts of Britain. Minus 20 degrees was recorded in Welshpool a few days later.

29th January, 1954

A Bristol housewife takes frozen shirts from her washing line.
2nd February, 1954

Just two of the millions of
people across America,
Europe and Asia witnessing
a total eclipse of the sun,
sensibly using smoked glass
to protect their eyes.
30th June, 1954

Actress Rachel Lofting with her two year old son on her shoulders as they join others at the Serpentine, Hyde Park, during a heatwave.
1st September, 1954

Perilously close to the edge of the Serpentine in Hyde Park, a Londoner in his deck chair makes sure that he can at least keep his feet cool.
1st September, 1954

Facing page: In a wintry and largely deserted Trafalgar Square, a boy feeds grateful pigeons.
4th January, 1955

Three year old Christopher Lockyear of West Wickham, enjoying the benefits of a heavy snowfall.
14th January, 1955

Heavy snow on Hampstead
Heath made skiing a viable
means of transport for
residents.
14th January, 1955

Attempts being made to clear at least the pitch markings at The Valley, before a referee's pitch inspection prior to Charlton Athletic's scheduled match against Manchester United.
15th January, 1955

Ice floes on the shore at Southport, washed up by the incoming tide, while arctic conditions prevail across much of Britain. In Scotland on the same day, Braemar records a temperature of minus 25 degrees, not quite equalling its own record low for the UK of minus 27.2 degrees.
23rd February, 1955

Facing page: Storm damage at Peacehaven, near Brighton in Sussex, following two days of south-westerly gales.
4th May, 1955

A nine month old at the Serpentine in Hyde Park works on his ice-cream technique.
13th July, 1955

Sally the chimpanzee is provided with an ice-cream cornet to cool her down in a heatwave.
14th July, 1955

An American serviceman
and a British fireman tip
rubble into a crane bucket
during clearance of many
tons of chalk at Ramsgate,
Kent, after heavy rains
seeped through the chalk
cliffs, causing a collapse.
22nd October, 1955

The statue in Piccadilly Circus, draped with icicles following a bitterly cold night with temperatures well below freezing. The statue depicts the god *Anteros*, not his brother *Eros* as is commonly believed.

1st February, 1956

Sheila Searle (L) and Penelope Gibbons, both from Richmond in Surrey, share a frozen pond on Wimbledon Common with a swan that seems to be wondering where the water has gone.
4th February, 1956

Arm in arm on Wimbledon
Common, skaters make the
most of the cold weather.
4th February, 1956

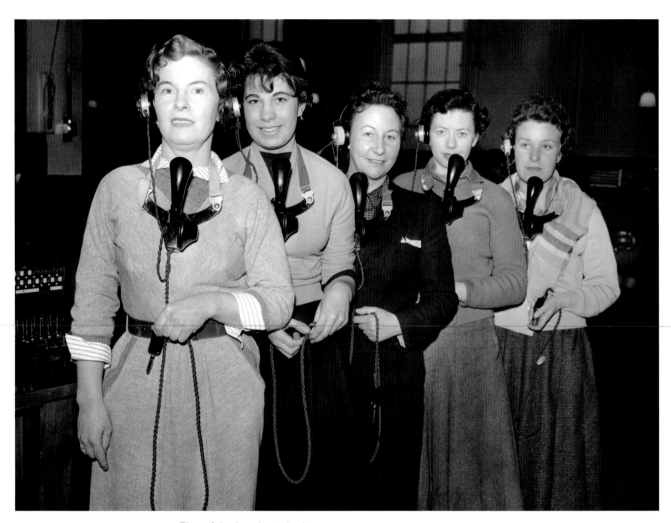

Five of the London telephone
operators who will operate
a new weather forecast-
by-telephone service, at
Holborn Exchange.
22nd February, 1956

A brick chimney stack is all that is left of the upper part of this council house in Love Lane, Aveley, Essex, after it had been struck by lightning.
17th April, 1956

Facing page: Norman Wisdom waits for rain to stop on the Woburn Abbey set of his film *Up in the World* in which he plays a window cleaner at a stately home. This was to become his fourth hit in as many years.
9th July, 1956

An umbrella is held aloft as Marilyn Monroe and her husband, playwright Arthur Miller, arrive in England from New York for filming of *The Prince and the Showgirl* at Pinewood Studios.
14th July, 1956

Guests scatter in all directions as a thunderstorm breaks over a Garden Party held by the Queen at Buckingham Palace.
19th July, 1956

Facing page: Weekend filming in the sunny streets of the City of London, as this actor portrays a Fleet Street reporter in the Ealing comedy *Barnacle Bill* with Alec Guinness.
16th June, 1957

Laden with pails and mopping-up cloths, three members of the catering staff paddle through a flooded Wimbledon Stadium. Floods caused greyhound racing to be postponed.

13th August, 1957

Three residents of Catford
brave floods in Waterbank
Road, caused by the swollen
River Ravensbourne.
13th August, 1957

Keeper Buck Jones and
Rusty the elephant mount
a combined operation to
clear snow from the elephant
enclosure at London Zoo.
21st January, 1958

Snow lends a winter
enchantment to the ancient
Derbyshire village of
Tissington, better known for
its springtime well-dressing
ceremony.
22nd January, 1958

Spurs beat Manchester City
5-1 in the mud, but headlines
still focus on the Munich
air disaster in the snow two
days previously, the tragedy
in which Manchester United
lost seven players along with
eight journalists and several
Club officials.
8th February, 1958

Facing page: The Biggin Hill
to Westerham road in Kent
is impassable due to deep
snow, as a local farmer tries
to free a car stuck in a ditch.
26th February, 1958

Facing page: The previous night's last service, still carrying passengers returning from a night out, is finally ready to continue its journey after being trapped by blizzards near Biggin Hill in Kent.
26th February, 1958

Groundsman Fred Eckersley, clearing deep snow around a goalmouth at Burnden Park where home side Bolton Wanderers hope to play Wolverhampton Wanderers in the sixth round of the FA Cup.
26th February, 1958

A few spectators with umbrellas, hoping that play might resume, stay on and brave the rain that stopped play in the British hard court tennis championships at Bournemouth.
24th April, 1958

Facing page: Ladies enjoy a spring heatwave in Hyde Park, London, while considering the merits of the latest fashions.
30th April, 1958

A miserable Wimbledon spectator gazes up at the rain clouds from beneath her umbrella. The year's tournament saw one of the wettest first weeks ever, but the eventual finals managed to finish on schedule.
28th June, 1958

Flooding drives people and their pets upstairs, while they keep a watch on the watery scene below in Friars Road, Chelmsford, Essex.
6th September, 1958

Facing page: Making the most of fine weather on Derby Day at Epsom, two spectators improvise grandstand seats while the rest of the crowd relax on the grass.
3rd June, 1959

Television dancer Sheila Atha mimes fun in the snow for the camera in one of Manchester's parks, between rehearsals.
10th January, 1959

Model Sheila McDonough
demonstrates the summer's
heat for the camera by frying
eggs on the roof of a car at
Seapoint, near Dublin.
23rd June, 1959

Knee-deep in floodwater, a determined milkman continues his rounds in Berkeley Close, Ruislip, Middlesex.

11th July, 1959

Avenues of pear blossom in the spring sunshine make a pleasant start to the day's duties at the Long Ashton Agriculture and Research Station at Bristol.
2nd May, 1960

Facing page: Implausibly, the thatched roof of this flood-damaged Devonshire cottage remains intact as its occupants search for their belongings in the water-logged rubble.
2nd October, 1960

Facing page: One of many Devon firemen engaged in flood rescue work helps a local resident to dry land.
7th October, 1960

A crumpled mass of thatch is all that remains of Exton Church in Devon after floodwaters undermined its foundations.
2nd October, 1960

Devon floods affect more than the local people as Mr and Mrs Howarth carry Rex, the family dog, and Dinah, their pet monkey, to safety.
7th October, 1960

A canoe paddled with
a piece of scrap timber
conveys these men along
one of Exmouth's flooded
streets while others settle
for getting their feet wet.
7th October, 1960

Arriving home from work in the dark, these residents of Exmouth are forced to use a small rowing boat to get to their homes along the town's flooded streets.
7th October, 1960

"Maybe the engine's flooded…" The River Waring at Horncastle, Lincolnshire, and a car which was swept several hundred yards from its parking place by floods caused by a sudden torrential downpour.

8th October, 1960

Facing page: Knee deep in water, residents of Romsey in Hampshire wade through the worst floods the town has seen for 70 years, with water eight feet deep in some places.
9th October, 1960

Largely submerged, a milk float is stranded in deep floods at Methley, near Leeds, Yorkshire.
27th November, 1960

Facing page: Police clad in waders unload provisions from a small boat in Southgate Street, Bath.
5th December, 1960

A bus ploughs its way through rising floodwaters on the main Newport-Cardiff road in the suburbs of the Welsh capital, following gale force winds and torrential rain.
4th December, 1960

After devastating floods,
Bath resembles Venice as
swans and their cygnets
glide majestically down
Southgate Street, the city's
main shopping thoroughfare.
5th December, 1960

Facing page: Valerie Krieger
(R) and Straube Skrun share
a cool drink at the Hyde
Park Lido when London's
temperatures climbed
towards 27 degrees.
30th June, 1961

Facing page: Five thousand
people sunbathe in Hyde
Park's Serpentine Lido in
the sweltering London heat.
At 4:00pm the temperature
reached 33.3 degrees,
equalling the previous record
of 3rd June, 1947.
1st July, 1961

Third Division players of
Queens Park Rangers train
in the snow beside a pitch
that is unplayable.
3rd January, 1962

Industrial heaters from RAF
Culdrose are employed to dry
out fishermen's cottages at
Newlyn, Cornwall, following
floods. The heaters are
manned by Naval ratings.
10th March, 1962

Facing page: Londoners
Irene McLinley of Woolwich
(L) and Maureen Rowe from
Kennington, sunbathe at the
Oasis Pool in Holborn during
a heatwave.
9th June, 1962

The faces of French President General Charles de Gaulle and German Chancellor Konrad Adenauer feature in a novelty barometer commemorating their joint endeavours for Franco-German reconciliation.
11th September, 1962

Facing page: Two gentlemen take a walk on a foggy Embankment in London. Though dense, the fog is safer to breathe than the historic pea-soupers which brought about the Clean Air Act, passed six years earlier.
4th December, 1962

Arsenal manager Billy Wright
and referee A J Sturgeon,
postponing Arsenal's match
due to a heavy covering of
snow on Highbury's pitch.
29th December, 1962

Brighton and Hove Albion fans, waiting to see their team play visitors Crystal Palace, watching from mounds of snow cleared from the pitch and piled on the terraces.
12th January, 1963

Facing page: When farmer Bill Maynard went to bed the previous night, this two-acre field near Exeter lay under water from the flooded river Exe. When he awoke, the water had gone leaving a crop of ice floes, carried downstream as the thaw set in.
8th February, 1963

Brighton and Hove Albion fans' enthusiasm is un-cooled, despite the snow on the terraces.
12th January, 1963

Facing page: Tottenham Hotspur players (L-R) Dave MacKay, Bill Brown, Jimmy Greaves and Terry Dyson peer into the White Hart Lane fog in search of opposing Manchester United players. The match was postponed because of poor visibility.
27th November, 1963

Disappointed members of the West Indies cricket team make light of the rain that put paid to their opening tour match against Worcester.
1st May, 1963

Traffic at a standstill in snow
on Western Avenue leading
into London.
4th March, 1965

Facing page: For the first time in the century, a whole Royal
Ascot programme is lost through heavy rain. At least this
couple can see the funny side as they rush away from The
Paddock through mud and puddles.
18th June, 1964

Facing page: Grim August weather as thunderstorms hit London, making life miserable for motorists and pedestrians alike.
20th August, 1965

Londoners enjoy lunch in spring sunshine at the Victoria Embankment gardens.
29th March, 1965

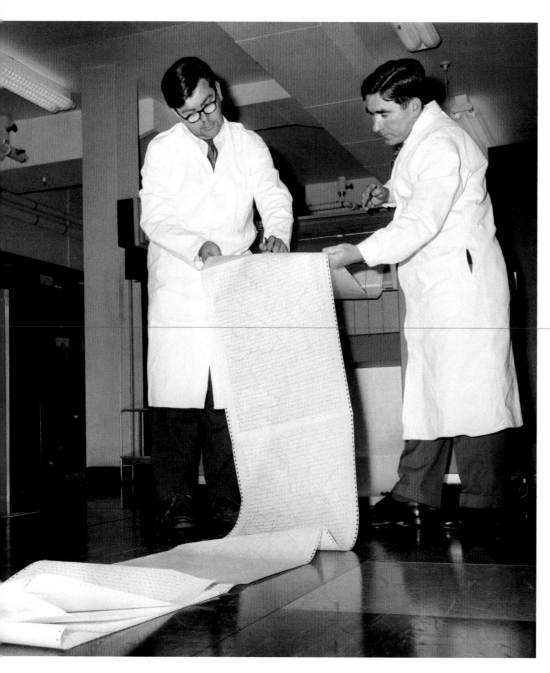

Operators of the Met Office's high-speed printer at Bracknell examine forecast charts, produced at 1,000 lines a minute. Teleprinter tapes of observations are received from the communications centre and fed directly into the computer, an English Electric Leo KDF9.

2nd November, 1965

A wall of sea water strikes Sandgate Road at Hythe in Kent, covering the promenade with pebbles to make driving even more precarious. Twenty years later, almost to the day, Hythe would again bear the brunt of atrocious weather as hurricane-force winds hit the south coast.

17th October, 1967

Facing page: A toddler is carried through Frankwell's swirling flood waters at Shrewsbury in Shropshire.
15th January, 1968

An intrepid cricket fan stays dry at Lord's during a rainstorm that made play impossible for much of the third day of the Second Test between England and Australia.
22nd June, 1968

Facing page: Two reporters for radio's *World At One*, Sue McGregor and Charles Stokes, attempt to fry an egg on the hot pavement of Piccadilly Circus, watched by understandably bemused bystanders.
2nd July, 1968

Three year old Erica takes a well-earned break from the exhausting autumnal task of sweeping up the dead leaves.
14th November, 1968

The Oasis swimming pool in Holborn, one of the few cool
spots among London's towering office blocks.
14th July, 1969

A Central Line tube train enters Epping Station during its
journey through a wintry Essex landscape.
4th March, 1970

A police motorcyclist is silhouetted by headlights as he tries to calm rush-hour chaos in Bristol. The thickest fog for many years, combined with voluntary switching off of street lighting to relieve an electricity shortage, caused traffic jams for several hours.

14th December, 1970

The sun finally proves too much for this Londoner, taking a nap under a newspaper near the Serpentine in Hyde Park.
14th July, 1972

Cooling off in the fountains
in Trafalgar Square is a good
solution to the heat for these
young Londoners.
10th June, 1975

Dress codes break down in a London heatwave, but this Fleet Street worker clings to his umbrella nonetheless.
8th August, 1975

Weather forecasters Jack
Scott and Barbara Edwards
showing new symbols
designed to give viewers a
clearer picture of the main
weather features, such as
sunshine, clouds, sleet, rain
and snow.
11th August, 1975

Space is at a premium in this scene on Brighton beach as temperatures climbed to 27 degrees. This summer was to be one of the hottest on record.

27th June, 1976

A depleted reservoir at
Staines in Middlesex, during
the severe drought of 1976,
lies cracked and empty
except for a shallow puddle
or two.
17th August, 1976

Ladybower Reservoir, near Bamford in Derbyshire, filled to the brim by heavy rainfall, generates a plughole effect as thousands of gallons of water are released into the valley below.
22nd February, 1977

Facing page: Despite a summer shower, the Queen greets crowds at Greenwich with a radiant smile before her Jubilee sail-about on the River Thames.
9th June, 1977

People salvage what they can from their beach huts at Herne Bay after a night of gales and high seas leave a trail of havoc. Dozens of people were evacuated from their homes.
12th January, 1978

The scene in St James' Park as October temperatures in London reach high summer levels.
12th October, 1978

Weather forecasters on a London rooftop celebrate the 25th anniversary of the weatherman on BBC television. BBC weather presenters are employed by the Meteorological Office, and assigned to tours of duty with the broadcaster.
9th January, 1979

The snowbound scene at Cannon Street Station spells bad news for the capital's commuters, already struggling to get into work on the third of a series of one-day rail strikes.
23rd January, 1979

Vehicles, tossed about like toys by massive seas which swept over Chesil Beach in Dorset, are left in an expensive heap on the shingle.

13th February, 1979

Almost May, yet motorists in
the Cotswolds faced snow
when the West Country bore
the brunt of arctic weather
sweeping down from
the north.
26th April, 1981

The River Severn floods
yet again, watched by two
small boys in Gloucester. It
will flood many more times
during their lifetimes.
2nd January, 1982

Sixty-eight year old amateur weather forecaster William Foggitt, from Thirsk in North Yorkshire, offers a long-range forecast for the forthcoming winter with the aid of seaweed and a fir cone.

2nd March, 1982

After the Trooping of the Colour, the Queen seems disconcerted by torrential rain as she canters back to Buckingham Palace.
12th June, 1982

The Queen, smiling despite the rain, on a walkabout at *HMS Warrior* in Northwood, Middlesex.
25th June, 1982

Eurovision Song Contest
entrants Sweet Dreams,
sharing a brolly in London.
They are: (L-R) Carrie Gray,
Bobby McVey and
Helen Cray.
23rd March, 1983

Eventual winner Michael Gratton (R) and Gerry Hulme in
the cooling rain of the 1983 London Marathon. The great
Norwegian runner, Ingrid Kristianson, won the women's race
and was to repeat her victory the following year.
1st April, 1983

On his last day at the Meteorological Office after 42 years, TV weatherman Jack Scott hedges his bets when predicting the outcome of the forthcoming General Election.

13th May, 1983

Princess Anne is prepared
for British Bank Holiday
weather, dressed in long
riding coat, Wellington boots
and sou'wester.
26th May, 1984

An aircraft is defrosted as heavy snowfalls are experienced for the second day running. During the next four days some parts of southern England would not climb above minus four degrees.
9th February, 1985

100 Years of Weather • Twentieth Century in Pictures

Facing page: Crowds are cooled with a hosepipe during the historic Live Aid concert at Wembley Stadium.
13th July, 1985

The Princess of Wales, dressed in characteristically eye-catching style, seeks shelter from the rain under a friend's umbrella at Royal Ascot.
17th June, 1987

An uprooted tree outside the Victoria and Albert Museum in London after 94mph winds hit the capital, during the 1987 hurricane famously not predicted by the Met Office. Eighteen people died. The last storm of similar ferocity occurred in 1703.

16th October, 1987

A car lies crushed by a fallen tree, one of 15m which were uprooted or severely damaged as hurricane-force winds ripped across southern England. Shanklin Pier, on the Isle of Wight, was reduced to driftwood and the Channel Islands recorded winds in excess of 110mph.

16th October, 1987

TV-am's weather girl Trish Williamson and the BBC's Ian McCaskill on the roof of the London Weather Centre, after McCaskill was voted Weather Person of the Year and Williamson runner up.
17th December, 1987

Ian McCaskill and a colleague prepare a BBC TV weather forecast in London, as a storm makes its way slowly across the country from the Atlantic.
9th February, 1988

Weathermen Bill Giles (L), Ian McCaskill and Michael Fish (R) make a fashion statement outside the BBC Television Centre to introduce new computerised weather displays.
20th May, 1988

TV weatherman Michael Fish uses the old-fashioned method to see if it's raining, on the roof of the Met Office's headquarters in Bracknell.
12th October, 1988

A saddened John Simmons, Curator of the Royal Botanical Gardens at Kew, stands beside a century-old Black Pine, one of 100 trees destroyed by gales at the world-famous botanic gardens in West London. Fortunately the damage was not as severe as that caused by the 1987 hurricane.
26th January, 1990

Spectators at the treacherously cobbled Hob Hole Ford, between Westerdale and Kildale Moors in North Yorkshire, witness Italian cyclist Andrea Tafi come unstuck during the 1990 Kellogg's Tour of Britain.
4th August, 1990

Father and daughter get airborne as snow hits Newark. Much of the Midlands experienced snowfall of up to eight inches deep, Birmingham receiving double that, while strong winds whipped up snowdrifts six feet deep in places.
8th December, 1990

Nicholas Gosling (L) and
brother Tim, enjoying a well-
timed heatwave with friends
Daryl Rayner (L) and Helen
Thomas at the Henley Royal
Regatta.
6th July, 1991

England's Ian Wright (L) and Paul Gascoigne at a training session in the run up to the World Cup qualifying match away to Turkey, where pitch conditions were unlikely to resemble those at home.
28th March, 1993

PC Neil Coward gives WPC
Teresa Bound a single red
rose in Valentine's Day snow.
14th February, 1994

Facing page: Sandhurst resident Alan Johnson and his three children escape from their marooned home near Gloucester, through floodwater that was up to five feet deep in places.
1st February, 1995

A United Nations Landrover is stuck in floodwaters as the Army and UN help out in Boroughbridge, Yorkshire, by ferrying people to safety. Meanwhile a local windsurfer demonstrates a more successful – if eccentric – form of flood transport.
1st February, 1995

York gets some of its
heaviest snow of the winter
months, its famed daffodil
display asserting that it is
really spring.
28th March, 1995

Families make the most of the weather on the beach
at Redcar during the last days of the school holiday,
unconcerned by the steelworks behind them.
22nd August, 1995

Squally showers and strong winds make Blackpool's Promenade a bleak place as the August Bank Holiday approaches, despite scorching sun during the previous weeks.
24th August, 1995

Feeder rivers for North West Water's reservoirs near Denshaw, at Saddleworth Moor, are reduced to a trickle as a long hot summer takes its toll.
26th August, 1995

Walking dogs in the North
Pennines, a pet owner
enjoys the first snowfall of
the winter on Killhope Moor.
16th November, 1995

Facing page: On the day
after Boxing Day, the mail
is delivered by sledge in the
village of Rillington, near
Malton in North Yorkshire.
27th December, 1995

The shores of Loch Morlich, near Aviemore in Scotland, where John Evans from Northampton takes the opportunity to run his dogs before the Winalot Husky Racing Championship, in Glenmore Forest.
18th January, 1996

Facing page: Football fans demonstrate their commitment in atrocious weather conditions to attend an FA Cup match in Nottingham.
19th February, 1996

After just 15 minutes, the FA Cup Fifth Round match
between Nottingham Forest and Spurs is abandoned as the
ground is subjected to a ferocious blizzard. The replayed
game was a draw, leading to a third match which Forest
eventually won on penalties.

19th February, 1996

A stranded driver checks
on the condition of her Mini,
almost completely buried in
a snowdrift near Dover, Kent.
21st February, 1996

A child tests the thickness of ice surrounding a fountain
draped in icicles in London's Trafalgar Square, following days
of falling temperatures in the capital.
22nd February, 1996

The cross of St George catches the light against a vivid sunset over Wembley Stadium, as England host a friendly against Croatia.
24th April, 1996

Facing page: Rain stops play again as England and India Test sides attempt to finish their three-match series despite appalling weather conditions.
25th May, 1996

A traditional bank holiday scene at Scarborough, with visitors packing the seaside resort in spite of poor weather that forced them to take umbrellas onto the beach.
26th May, 1996

Early summer fun for these children on the beach at Weymouth as the weather finally improves at the end of the May half-term holiday week.
30th May, 1996

England's Paul Gascoigne on the receiving end of refreshment from Teddy Sheringham after scoring a sublime goal, England's second, in the Euro 96 Group A game against Scotland. England won 2-0 and went on to win the Group.

15th June, 1996

Changeable weather during Wimbledon brings out the covers,
meaning interruptions throughout the championships.
A rainbow provides a reminder of the pot of gold awaiting
the winner.
1st July, 1996

The A66 trunk road from Scotch Corner to Penrith, usually one of the first routes over the Pennines to be affected by wintry conditions, receives its first snowfall of the year.
18th November, 1996

Concern for the elderly is highlighted as snow and freezing weather persist, with the Government's handling of cold weather payments attracting criticism.
2nd January, 1997

Warm sunshine and blue skies add to the colour of a display of daffodils along York's city walls, where these two youngsters enjoy the sharp contrast to the blizzards of the previous month.
10th April, 1997

London's St James' Park,
when temperatures in
the capital climbed above
16 degrees.
30th May, 1997

With 50 years in the umbrella manufacturing business, Arnold Miller of Walsall is delighted as unusually poor weather brings a boost in sales.
27th June, 1997

Facing page: Even the
scarecrow takes cover as
it stands guard over a crop
flattened by rain near York.
The previous month was the
wettest June in England and
Wales of the 20th century.
1st July, 1997

A small boy and his dog
cool off in the fountains of
Trafalgar Square as August
temperatures continue to soar.
19th August, 1997

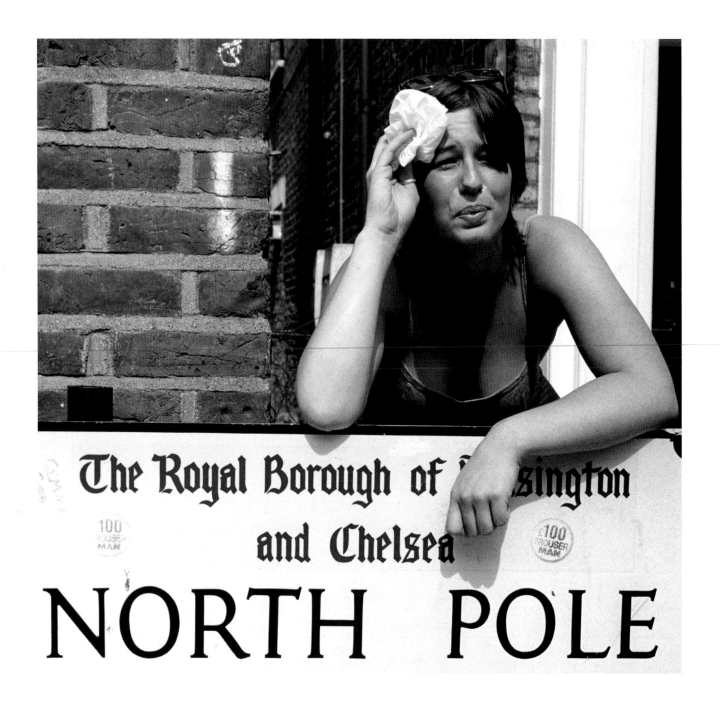

The Royal Borough of Kensington and Chelsea

NORTH POLE

Facing page: The *other* North Pole: temperatures across Britain hover around 30 degrees, with forecasters predicting the hottest August since records began.
20th August, 1997

Enthusiastic Tromsø fans help to clear snow from their home pitch in Norway in the hope that the Second Round European Cup Winners' Cup match against Chelsea can go ahead.
23rd October, 1997

As temperatures in the capital reach 25 degrees Londoners are warned of the 'heat island' effect, in which buildings and paved areas trap heat, causing higher than usual incidences of heatstroke.
6th August, 1998

Facing page: Spectacular, but not untypical, conditions at Glastonbury Festival.
27th June, 1998

Bournemouth beach is packed as temperatures soar and statistics reveal the true cost of sun worship. More than 50% suffer sunburn with 12% experiencing blistered skin. As many as 30% are happy with temperatures of up to 32 degrees, while 6% are prepared to see the thermometer hit 38 degrees.

10th August, 1998

Facing page: For the second time in a week, gale force winds create havoc and the trams on Blackpool seafront are towed to safety from the exceptionally high tides. Earlier in the week eight people lost their lives as severe gales caused damage costing millions of pounds.

1st February, 2002

Passengers at Stansted Airport wait for information on cancelled flights. Freezing conditions created traffic chaos and prompted criticism of the Highways Agency for failing to respond to earlier predictions. The Automobile Association reported three times the usual number of emergency calls, with some motorists stuck in their cars on the M11 for 20 hours.
31st January, 2003

Facing page: Newcastle is bathed in sunshine as Easter approaches. While an estimated 1.75m British holidaymakers were preparing for Easter abroad, those opting to stay at home were promised gorgeous spring weather with temperatures topping 16 degrees.
29th March, 2002

Facing page: Four gentlemen enjoy April sunshine on St Stephens Green, Dublin, although temperatures rose to only 14 degrees due to breezes off the Irish Sea.
18th April, 2003

Jenny the donkey takes a break with an ice cream before returning to the toil of carrying children along Weston-Super-Mare's beach on a hot afternoon.
10th August, 2003

Stirling Castle shrouded in early morning autumn mist. The castle's elevated position, dominating the lowest crossing point of the River Forth, has been attacked or besieged at least 16 times during its 900-year history.
29th October, 2003

Winter in the Scottish
Borders can't be easy for
farmers, but some calves
just aren't helping.
21st December, 2003

Easter holidaymakers, encouraged by mild temperatures, take periodic showers in their stride on Brighton beach.
10th April, 2004

Facing page: Bournemouth beach hut owners enjoy an exceptionally mild Easter. Throngs of daytrippers head for the resort during a month of above average temperatures.
11th April, 2004

Gale force winds batter
the Kent coastline. Heavy
winds heralded the arrival
of torrential rain as the
Highways Agency advised
motorists not to travel unless
absolutely necessary.
7th July, 2004

A dramatic sunset over
The Racecourse Ground at
Wrexham promises a fine
day to follow the second-leg
UEFA Cup match against
Östers in the First Qualifying
Round.
29th July, 2004

Visitors to Brighton dive
from the sea wall to cool
off as temperatures climb.
Although this August proved
to be an unusually wet
month, sunshine totals were
close to average.
1st August, 2004

Facing page: A rain-
drenched August affects
retail sales everywhere, a
later study by the British
Retail Consortium declaring
it the slowest month of
the year.
5th August, 2004

REGENT · ARCADE

The Cornish village of Boscastle provides some of the most dramatic weather images of the decade as a wall of water devastates the tourist spot following almost eight inches of rain in 24 hours. Emergency services mount a massive rescue operation.
17th August, 2004

Saltcoats seafront is no
place for an umbrella
while high winds batter the
Ayrshire coast. Elsewhere in
Britain, conditions were more
subdued than the previous
day that had seen severe
gales across the south
of England.
11th November, 2005

An early morning jog across
Clifton Downs in Bristol,
beneath a canopy of autumn
colour and shrouded in mist.
6th November, 2006

A tornado tore briefly through the suburbs of London, ripping open this house on the corner of Chamberlayne Road and Whitmore Gardens. Although lasting for just 10 seconds winds reached 110mph, damaging 150 properties and leaving several families homeless for Christmas.
8th December, 2006

Spring flowers in Whitley Bay are decorated with a late carpet of snow as wintry weather lingers.
20th March, 2007

Facing page: A Highland cow is buried in snow at Carronbridge near Denny in Scotland after a heavy fall. Despite a cold snap lasting several days, the month was appreciably warmer than average.
18th January, 2007

Facing page: The
Postmaster of Toll Bar, near
Doncaster, clad in waders
to leave his flooded Post
Office. Floods caused by
the River Don were among
the worst in the country.
1st July, 2007

A freak hailstorm hits
London on a July afternoon,
delighting Sarah Schnell
from New Zealand who has
never seen hail before.
3rd July, 2007

Facing page: The footwork
might leave a little to be
desired, but people are
determined to enjoy *T in
the Park* at Balado, Perth
and Kinross, despite muddy
conditions underfoot.
6th July, 2007

An aerial view of Tewkesbury
Abbey in Gloucestershire,
following 24 hours of
torrential rain, dramatically
captures the impact and
isolation of flooding. Not far
away, RAF Brize Norton
recorded four inches of rain
in just seven hours.
22nd July, 2007

Gloucester residents suffer
the persistent floodwaters
of the River Severn.
24th July, 2007

Wind and rain lash Westminster Bridge during an unusually varied month in which temperatures ranged from 18.8 degrees in Sussex to minus 7.4 degrees in Cumbria.

15th November, 2007

Manchester's reputation for wet weather prompted the
Observer headline '*Tevez and Ronaldo reign in the rain*'
after United beat Derby County 4-1 in a drenched encounter,
typified by this shot of Tyrone Mears and Wayne Rooney.
8th December, 2007

Tewkesbury is affected by continued flooding across Britain. The town was still recovering from severe floods experienced during the previous July.

16th January, 2008

Toton Sidings, Nottinghamshire. The Green Belt area between the Sidings and the village of Bramcote is threatened by a study to identify sites suitable for 'Sustainable Urban Extension'.
10th February, 2008

After an earlier fog covering much of the country has lifted, two rutting red deer stags at Lotherton Hall near Wakefield provide the only colour in a frosty landscape.
20th February, 2008

A park at Burton on Trent, Staffordshire, during the highest average temperature for the first ten days of May since records began in 1772.
10th May, 2008

Wimbledon spectators – and staff – relax in the summer sunshine between matches. The previous day Andy Murray had staged a spectacular late comeback against Ricard Gasquet to set up a semi-final contest with Rafael Nadal.
1st July, 2008

As heavy rain falls over London, forecasters warn that some areas could experience up to three-quarters of the month's average rainfall in one day.
9th July, 2008

A thick carpet of autumn
leaves provides the
foreground as a dog-walker
enjoys a stroll through Great
Barr's Red House Park in
West Bromwich.
16th November, 2008

The Publishers gratefully acknowledge Press Association Images, from whose extensive archive the photographs in this book have been selected. Personal copies of the photographs in this book, and many others, may be ordered online at www.prints.paphotos.com

AMMONITE
PRESS

**PRESS
ASSOCIATION
Images**

For more information, please contact:
Ammonite Press
AE Publications Ltd. 166 High Street, Lewes, East Sussex, BN7 1XU, United Kingdom
Tel: 01273 488005 Fax: 01273 402866
www.ammonitepress.com